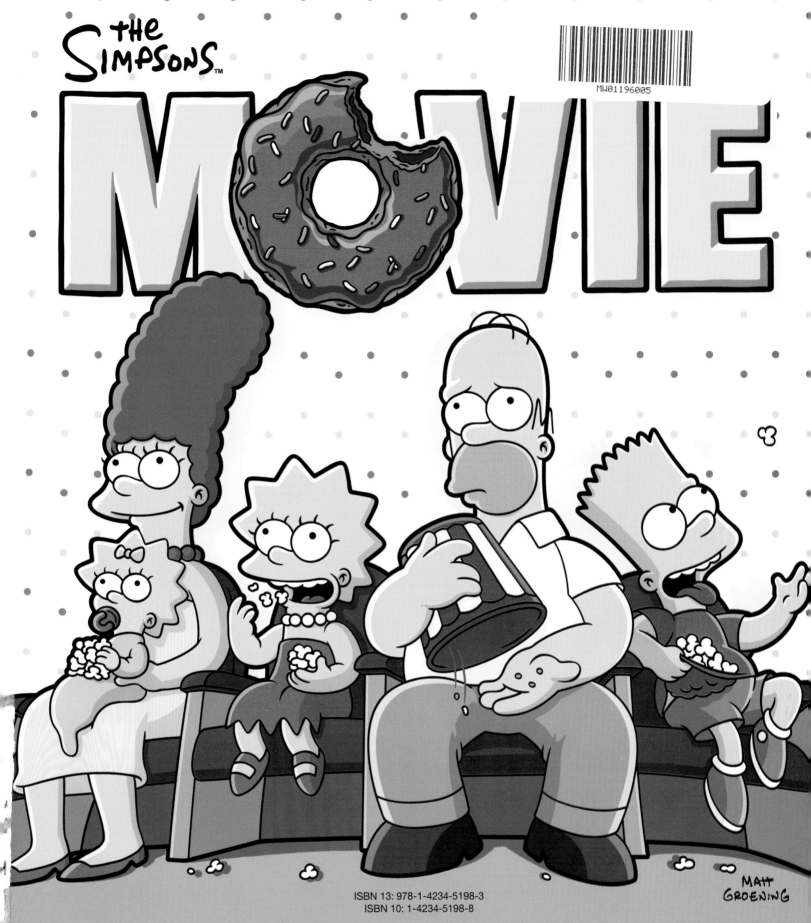

ISBN 13: 978-1-4234-5198-3
ISBN 10: 1-4234-5198-8

In Australia Contact:
Hal Leonard Australia Pty. Ltd.
4 Lentara Court
Cheltenham, Victoria, 3192 Australia
Email: ausadmin@halleonard.com

7777 W. BLUEMOUND RD. P.O. BOX 13819 MILWAUKEE, WI 53213

Visit Hal Leonard Online at
www.halleonard.com

CONTENTS

MATT GROENING

THEME FROM THE SIMPSONS™

Music by
DANNY ELFMAN

Moderately fast

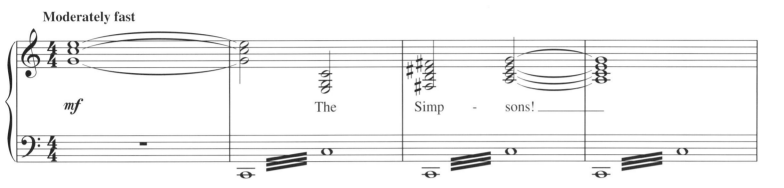

TRAPPED LIKE CARROTS

By HANS ZIMMER,
JAMES MICHAEL DOOLEY, ATLI ORVARSSON,
HENRY JACKMAN, LORNE BALFE,
RYELAND ALLISON, MICHAEL A. LEVINE
and DANNY ELFMAN

Slowly

Quickly

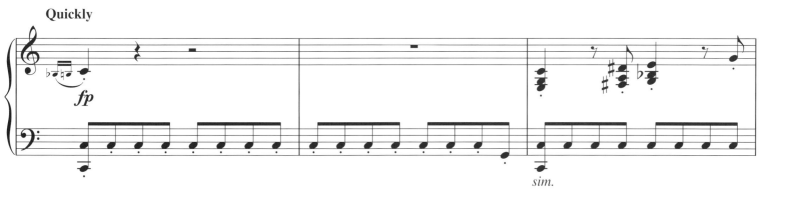

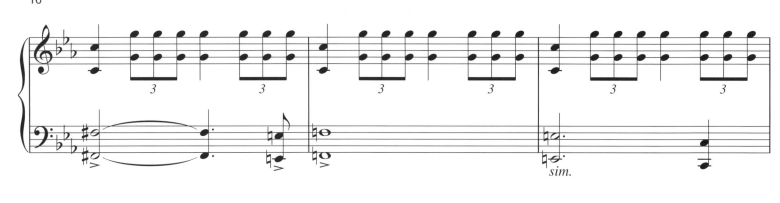

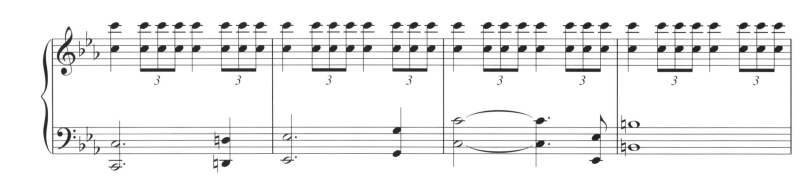

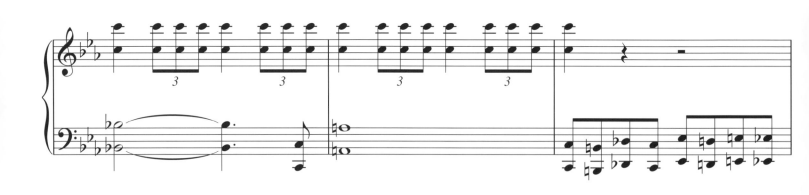

CLAP FOR ALASKA

By HANS ZIMMER,
JAMES MICHAEL DOOLEY, ATLI ORVARSSON,
HENRY JACKMAN, LORNE BALFE,
RYELAND ALLISON, MICHAEL A. LEVINE
and DANNY ELFMAN

Slowly, with freedom

With motion

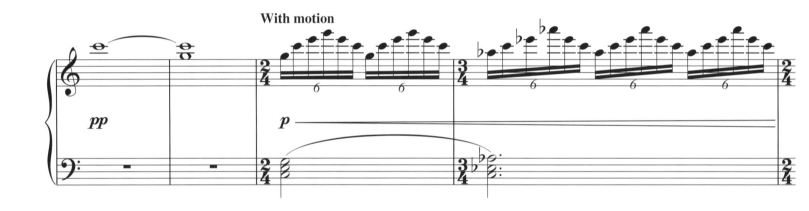

Very slowly

DOOMSDAY IS FAMILY TIME

By HANS ZIMMER
and DANNY ELFMAN

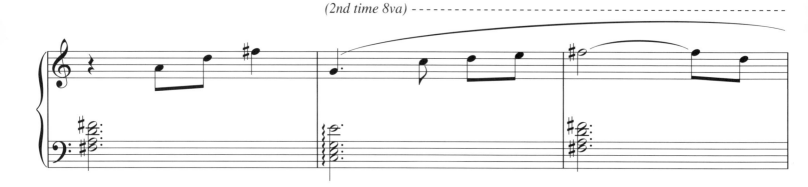

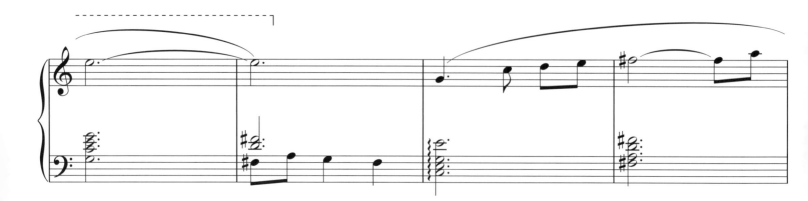

WHAT'S AN EPIPHANY?

By Hans Zimmer,
James Michael Dooley, Atli Orvarsson,
Henry Jackman, Lorne Balfe,
Ryeland Allison, Michael A. Levine
and Danny Elfman

Moderately slow

p

With pedal

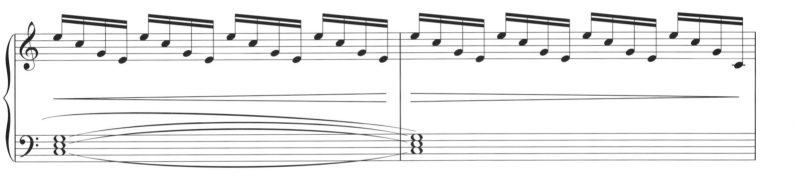

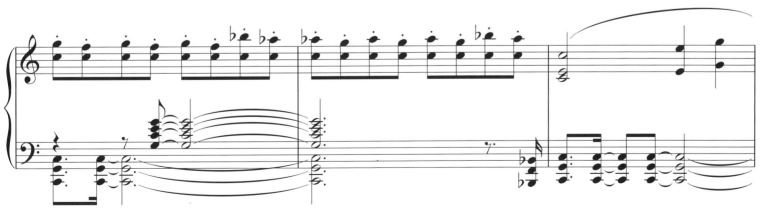

THANK YOU BOOB LADY

By HANS ZIMMER,
JAMES MICHAEL DOOLEY, ATLI ORVARSSON,
HENRY JACKMAN, LORNE BALFE,
RYELAND ALLISON, MICHAEL A. LEVINE
and DANNY ELFMAN

Moderately

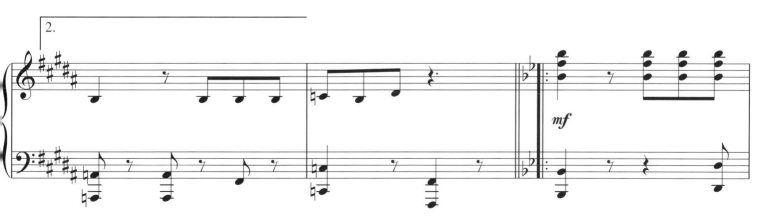

YOU DOOMED US ALL...AGAIN

By HANS ZIMMER,
JAMES MICHAEL DOOLEY, ATLI ORVARSSON,
HENRY JACKMAN, LORNE BALFE,
RYELAND ALLISON, MICHAEL A. LEVINE
and DANNY ELFMAN

Moderately

With pedal

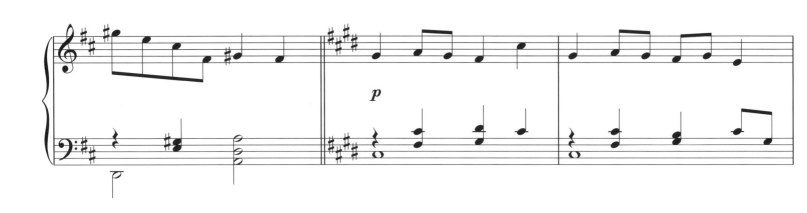

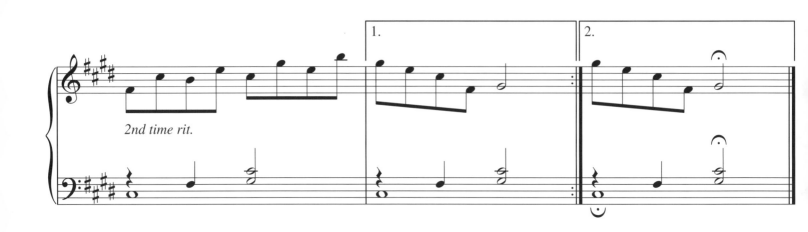

2nd time rit.

BART'S DOODLE

By MICHAEL A. LEVINE

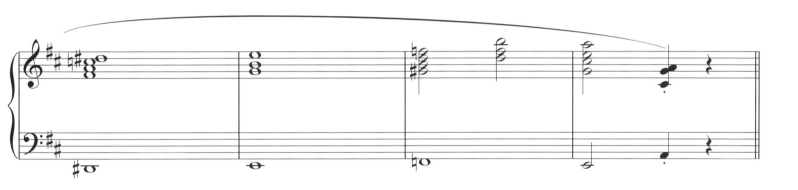

WORLD'S FATTEST FERTILIZER SALESMAN

By HANS ZIMMER
and DANNY ELFMAN

Moderately slow

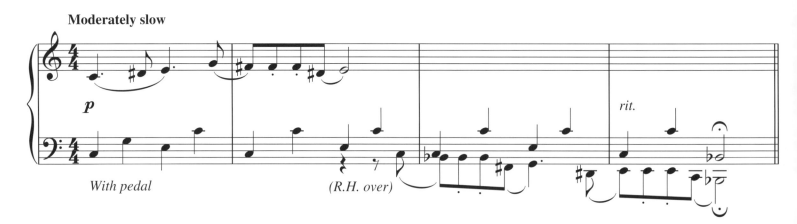

Quickly

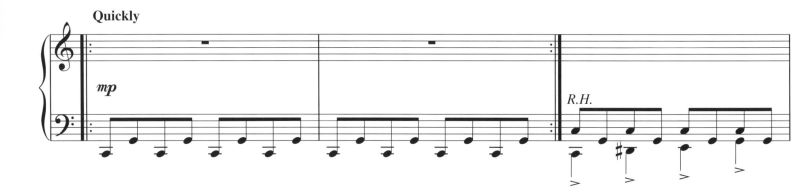

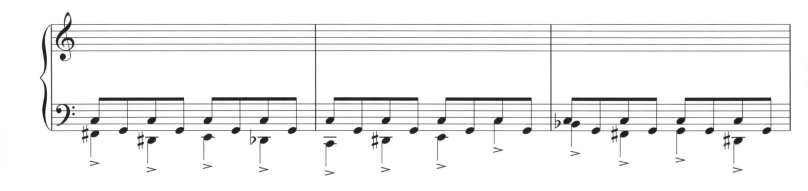

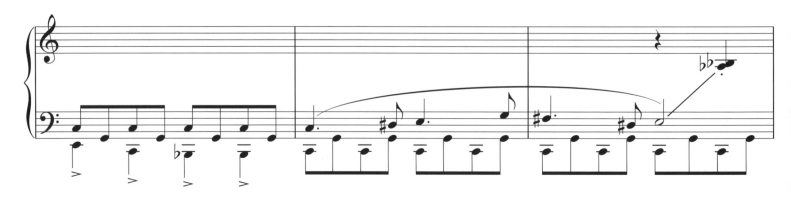

HIS BIG FAT BUTT COULD SHIELD US ALL

By HANS ZIMMER,
JAMES MICHAEL DOOLEY, ATLI ORVARSSON,
HENRY JACKMAN, LORNE BALFE,
RYELAND ALLISON and MICHAEL A. LEVINE

Slowly and freely

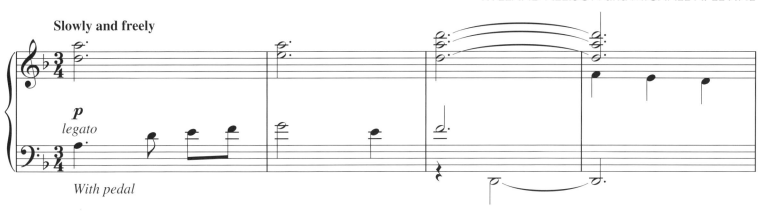

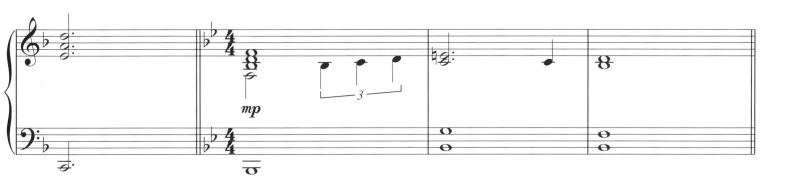

Gently

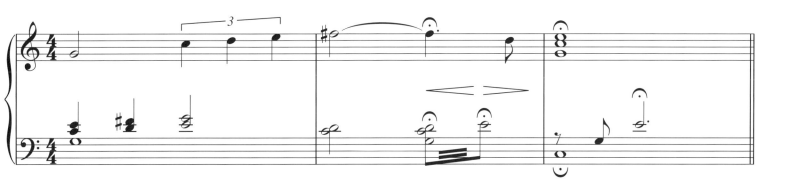

Moving quickly

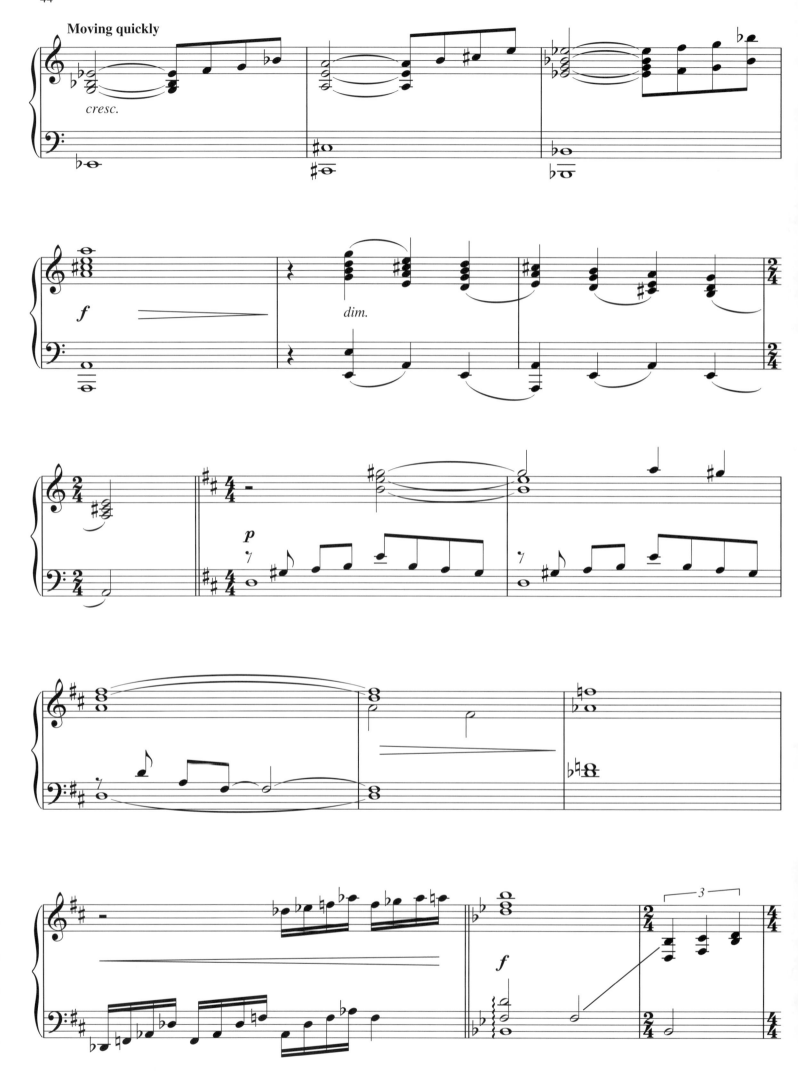

SPIDER PIG

Based on the composition "Theme from Spiderman"
written by PAUL FRANCIS WEBSTER and BOB HARRIS
Parody Lyrics by JAMES I. BROOKS,
MATT GROENING, AL JEAN, IAN MAXTONE GRAHAM,
GEORGE MEYER, DAVID MIRKIN, MIKE REISS,
MIKE SCULLY, MATT SELMAN,
JOHN SWARTZWELDER and JON VITTI

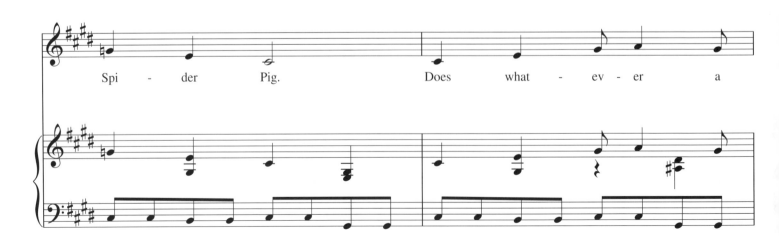